I'm Reading About

VERMONT

The Green Mountain State!

GALLOPADE

by Carole Marsh

Printed and Manufactured in Peachtree City, GA., USA
www.gallopade.com

Book design: John Hanson

Editorial manager: Janice Baker

Vermont is a great state.

It is one of a kind.

What makes Vermont special?

Let's read about it

and see!

NATIVE AMERICANS

Who lived in Vermont first?

Native Americans did!

They moved around to find food.
They hunted in Vermont's woods.
They fished in Vermont's rivers.
They gathered fruits and seeds and nuts.

EXPLORERS

The first explorers came to Vermont in 1609.
They came from the country of France.

Samuel de Champlain was their leader.
He and his men were looking for new land!

SETTLEMENT

Colonists from Massachusetts came into Vermont.
They started the first permanent settlement
in Vermont in 1724.
They named it Fort Dummer.

Fort Dummer is located in the
town of Brattleboro today.

Fort Dummer

Artist's Conception of Original Fort Dummer

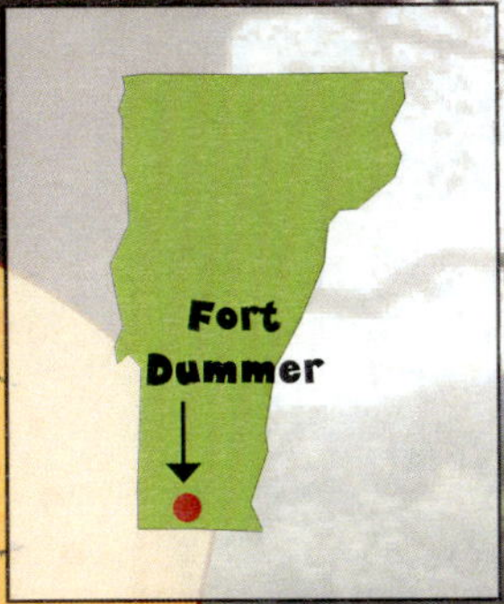

STATEHOOD

Vermont was the 14th state to join the United States of America!

Isn't it great,
to be a state!
I bet Vermont
could hardly wait!

Vermont became a state in 1791.

Vermont
The 14th State
Here we are!

FLAG

I am the state flag.
I was adopted in 1923.

What color am I?
I am blue.

Look at me.
What else do you see?

I fly high over the state of Vermont!

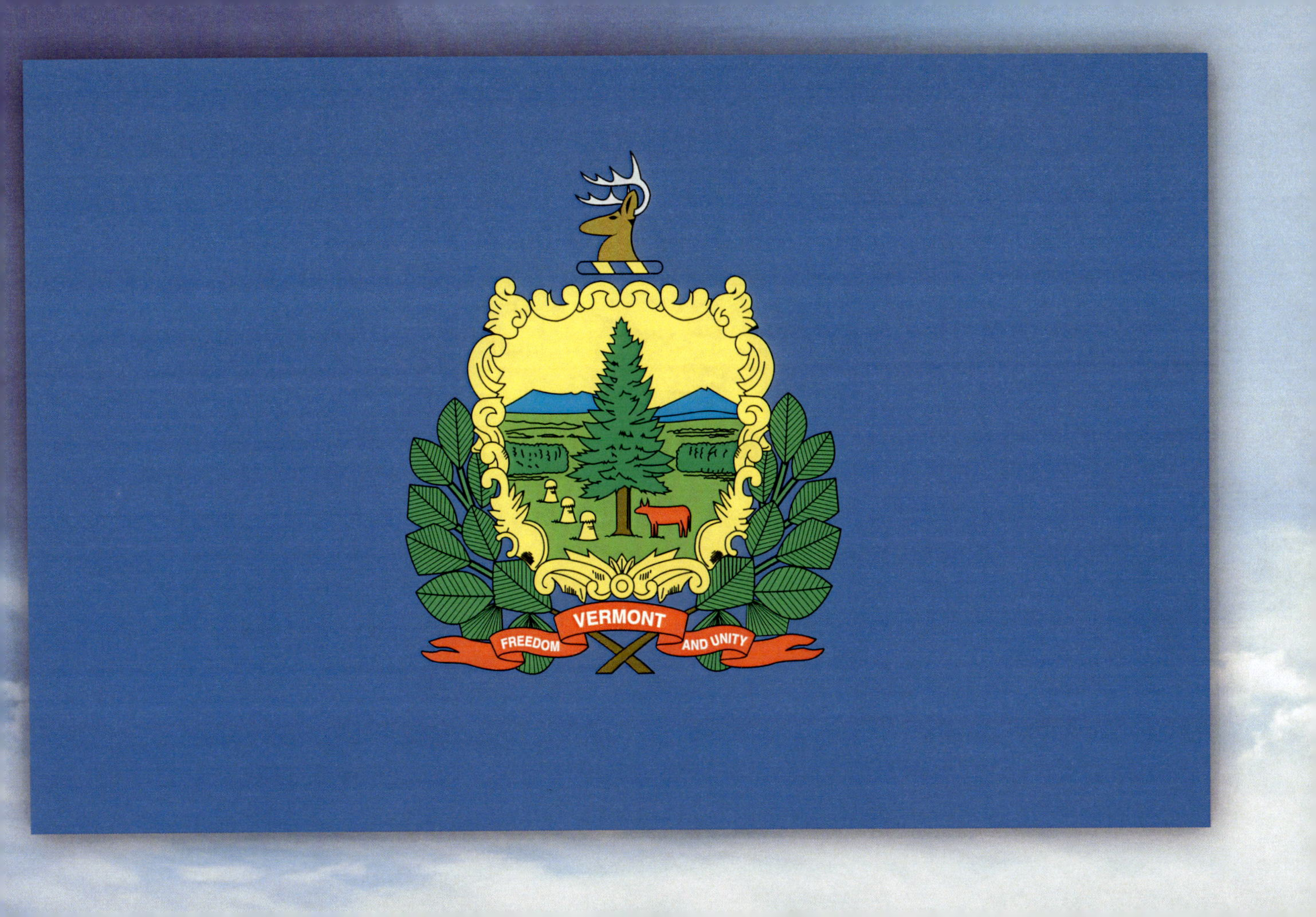
VERMONT
FREEDOM
AND UNITY

CAPITAL

Say hello to Montpelier,
the capital city of Vermont!

There is an important building in Montpelier.
It is the State House.
Vermont's laws are made there!

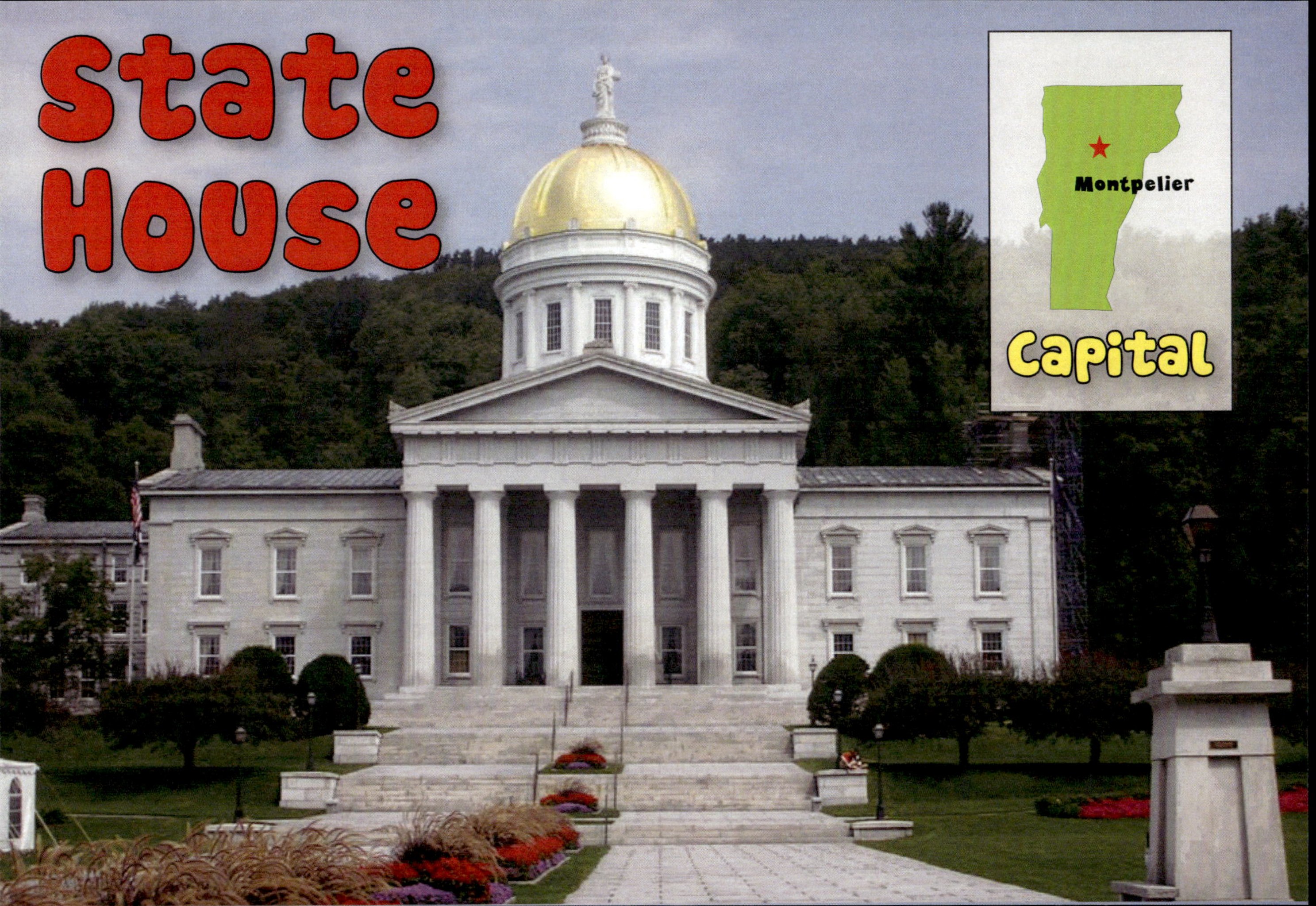
State House
Montpelier
Capital

SEAL

I am a seal,
but I am not the State Seal.
If I were, I would be very important.
I would be stamped on many official papers.
(Ouch, that might hurt!)

VERMONT
FREEDOM & UNITY
Now, that's official!

NICKNAME

State nicknames are fun!
State nicknames are great!
They share fun facts
about each state!

Vermont's nickname is "The Green Mountain State."

Vermont's mountains are covered in green trees!

The Green Mountain State

BORDERS

Look at Vermont.
Vermont is in a region called "the Northeast."

Vermont borders three other states.
It also borders the country of Canada.
Find Vermont and its neighbors on the map!

Vermont comes from French words that mean "green mountains."

Borders

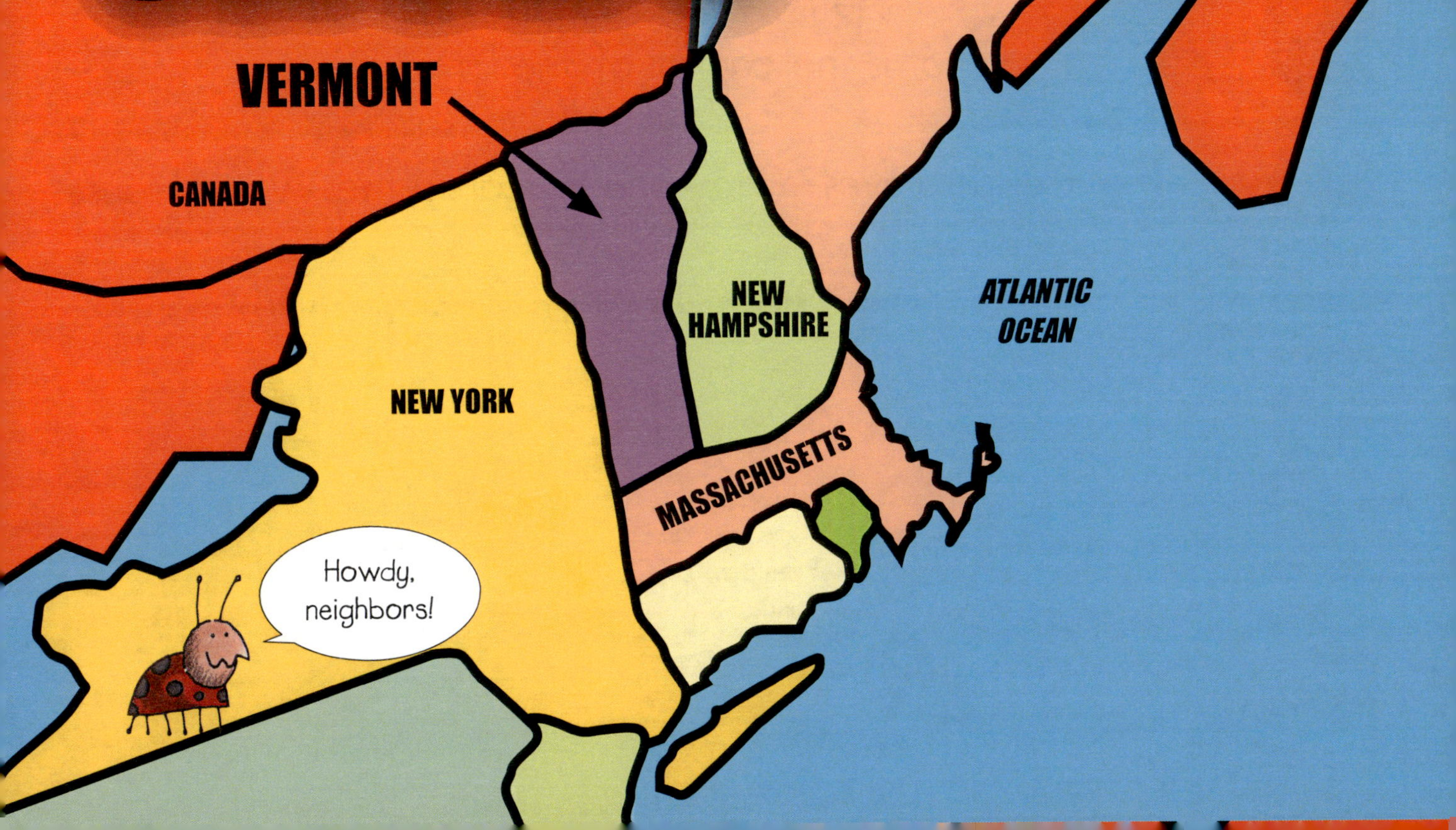
VERMONT
CANADA
NEW HAMPSHIRE
ATLANTIC OCEAN
NEW YORK
MASSACHUSETTS
Howdy, neighbors!

PRESIDENTS

The President is the leader of our country.
He lives in Washington, D.C.
That is the capital of the United States.

The President lives in a big house called the White House.

Several United States Presidents are from Vermont!

Chester A. Arthur
21st President

Calvin Coolidge
30th President

PEOPLE

Many famous people

Ethan Allen

Leader of the Green Mountain Boys in the American Revolution

John Deere

Invented the steel plow

Henry David Lee

Created Lee Jeans

call our state home!

Grace Anna Coolidge
First Lady and wife of President Calvin Coolidge

Roger Easton
Invented the Global Positioning System (GPS)

Ben Cohen and Jerry Greenfield
Creators of Ben and Jerry's Ice Cream

Hermit Thrush

BIRD

I am the state bird, and I fly
over Vermont, proud and high.

As I fly, up in the sky,
I flap my wings to tell you "Hi!"

The Vermont state bird is the Hermit Thrush.

Red Clover

FLOWER

I am the Red Clover.
I am the state flower.

I grow where it's warm and sunny.
I bloom in spring and summer.
I help make Vermont beautiful!

Look at me! Smell me!
Some people use red clover
to make tea!

Sugar Maple

TREE

I am a Sugar Maple—I'm the state tree.
All over Vermont is where to find me.

My roots run deep, they keep me strong.
I can live for hundreds of years—that's very long!

I stand up straight, big and tall.
Don't climb too high—it would hurt to fall!

Honeybee

INSECT

I am the Honeybee.
I am the state insect.

I might sting you if you bother me.
But really, I am your friend.

I carry pollen from flower to flower.
I make honey.
I help Vermont crops grow.

BZZZZZZZZZZZZ!

Lakes

LAKES

Let's go to the lake!

We can wade in the water.
We can ride on a boat.

We can jump off the dock
onto an inner tube float!

Vermont's lakes are home to many animals:

Fish **Snakes** **Birds** **Turtles** **Salamanders** **and More!**

Green Mountains

Vermont's Green Mountains are the place to be.
Hiking, fishing, camping—
fun for you and me.

If you were to climb
to the top of a tree,
you'd have a very nice view to see!

Rivers

RIVERS

Vermont has many rivers.
People like to use rivers for boating and fishing.

The river habitat is home to many animals:

Birds Deer Snakes Frogs Fish and More!

Rivers were Vermont's first highways.
Early settlers traveled along Vermont's rivers.
They also used the rivers to send logs downstream!

Bennington Battle Monument

LANDMARK

The Bennington Battle Monument
is the tallest structure in Vermont!
It is a symbol of the Battle of Bennington.
The battle took place during the American Revolution.

Visitors can ride an elevator to the
top of the tower.
They can see three states—New York,
Massachusetts, and Vermont!

Vermont Crops

AGRICULTURE

Vermont has many farms.
Why?
Because Vermont has good soil and a mild climate!

Some of the top crops produced in Vermont are:

Hay **Maple Syrup** **Apples** **Corn**

Hey!
Don't forget about me!
I am a Vermont cow.
I produce lots of milk to make dairy products!
Mooooooooo!

Sports in Vermont

Basketball! Ice Hockey! Soccer! Lacrosse!
Vermont has it all.

Whether you like to watch or play,
you are sure to have a ball!

Catamounts

Purple Knights

Panthers

& More!

Vermont: Home of Maple Syrup
It's so sticky, but so good!
Let's make pancakes!

CLAIM TO FAME

Vermont is known for its maple syrup!
Vermont produces the most maple syrup
of any U.S. state.
Sugar Maple trees produce sap.
Maple syrup is made from that tree sap!

People drill holes into the bark of
maple trees to collect the sap.

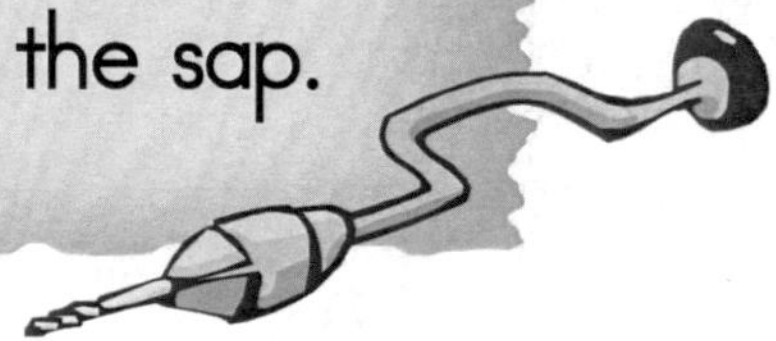

GLOSSARY

climate: weather conditions in an area over a long period of time

downstream: in the direction of a stream's current

elect: to choose someone by voting

elevator: a platform or compartment raised and lowered to move people or goods in a building

GPS: a navigation system that uses signals from satellites to tell you where you are and to give you directions to other places

habitat: a place where plants or animals naturally live

pollen: a yellow powder that helps plants make new plants

region: an area that has similar characteristics